Mudley

Explores

SINGAPORE

An Amazing Adventure in the Lion City

Arp Raph Broadhead

Marshall Cavendish
Editions

I can't believe this island has so much to write about, draw and photograph.
Can I pull it off?
We'll see, Mudley, we'll see!!

I belong to a little girl called Sophie. She lives in a small town in Europe. She would love to travel the world but she has to attend school and do her homework. And so, each time her dad has to leave for work at faraway places, she packs me into his suitcase and tells him, "Daddy. Please take Mudley along to see the world".

IMMIGRATION SINGAPORE
VISIT PASS
Subject to Reg. 12 (7)
Immigration Regulations
- 15 APR 2016
PERMITTED TO ENTER AND
REMAIN IN SINGAPORE
FOR A VISIT OF DAYS FOR
SOCIAL VISIT ONLY FROM
DATE SHOWN ABOVE

Mudley
Explores
SINGAPORE
An Amazing Adventure in the Lion City

Hello friend(s)!
Welcome to the secret world of Mudley.
Sophie thinks she is sending me on her personal mission but I have far more important
things to do than be someone's messenger. I have a secret ambition to be an artist
and these world travels are perfect opportunities for me to be inspired and achieve
my lifelong dream of exhibiting in an art gallery!

Don't forget passport !!!

Let me show you the Lion City or Singapore, an spectacular city that grew from
the riverbed. These pages are my paw prints from a fantastic journey seen
through my eyes, a journey that taught me so much about wonderful Singapore.

A view of the Fullerton Building, but what's surprising is the sculpture I'm seated on that looks like raindrops. I just wish they were, it's so hot!

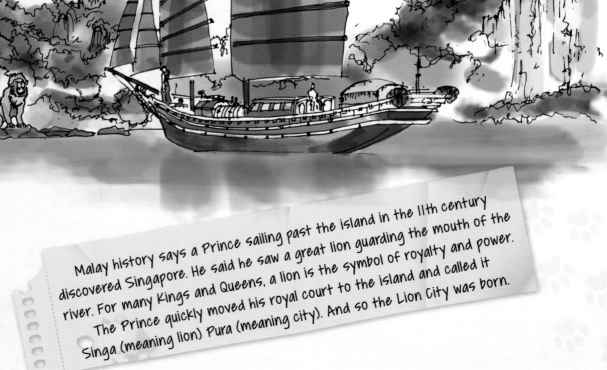

Malay history says a Prince sailing past the island in the 11th century discovered Singapore. He said he saw a great lion guarding the mouth of the river. For many Kings and Queens, a lion is the symbol of royalty and power. The Prince quickly moved his royal court to the island and called it Singa (meaning lion) Pura (meaning city). And so the Lion City was born.

I got a real soaking from Mr Funny Guy, the Merlion.

THE MERLION

I came straight here to see a friend of mine.
You can't miss him because he is over 8 metres tall. Say hello to the Merlion!
This is the iconic mascot of Singapore. He's half fish, half lion and he guards who comes
and goes up the Singapore River. So be good or else he will spray you with water.

Actually I really came to talk to the Merlion Cub as he is more friendly and more my size.
The Cub looks towards what was once a large fortress called Fort Fullerton, but that is no longer there.
Today in its place is the beautiful Fullerton Hotel, which was once the main post office on the island.

Welcome to Spikey!

Can you see me hanging? Look how this building keeps the sunlight out.

The Esplanade

This is not a fruit! Although the magnificent Esplanade looks like the famous durian fruit from South-East Asia, it is actually a theatre and concert hall. The whole building is magical both on the outside and the inside. It's special in many ways. The triangles you see on the roof let daylight in but keep the sun out, and there is a pipe organ that has a whopping 4,740 pipes. Wow, I really want to listen to the organ being played. Tonight I'm going to see a concert so this great place might just get better. See you later ...

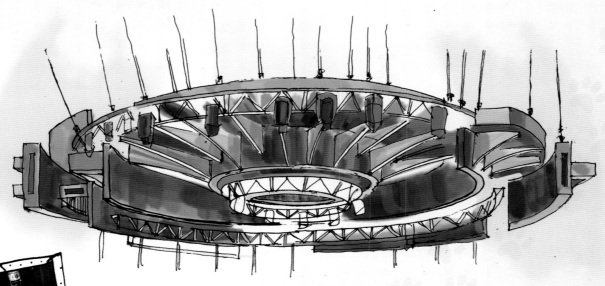

What a pong! These durian's really do smell.

Do you know what acoustics are? Acoustics in a theatre are its most important part. You wouldn't want to hear music that echoed because that would spoil the sound. Acoustics, good acoustics, make it possible for us to hear speech and music clearly. So a trained 'acoustician' is brought into theatres to make sure the only thing you hear are the words of the actors or the music. And here at the Esplanade Theatre, they have created a very special canopy that directs sound perfectly. The canopy goes up and down so you can tell if it's a mouse or an elephant singing. Clever! :)

Surprise, surprise,
I went off to Raffles Place only
to find a table tennis table.
I don't know how to play
but I love the orange table.

What Mr Raffy saw when he landed in Singapore was an ideal location for a trading port. But how could he acquire permission from the Sultan who was out of the country at the time? He met up with the Sultan's eldest brother who had no power at all, and told him he was the real Sultan of Singapore. Then he got the Sultan's brother to sign a contract to use the land. The little devil!

You were a bit
cunning Mr Raffy ...

A lot of places

STAMFORD RAFFLES

You may wonder why you see this name all over the place, and SO DID I!
Thomas Stamford Raffles was an adventurer, a colonial official, a linguist and, I am glad to say,
a very funny man. He is said to be the founding father of modern Singapore but he had to
battle hard for Singapore's position as an important trading port and be part of a shipping route.
He planned out a new city, wrote out laws for everyone living there and worked towards keeping
Singapore a multi-ethnic society. He was very interested in and enthusiastic about every aspect
of life in East Asia. It's funny though that his longest stay here in Singapore was just eight months.

Finally, a cricket pitch made just for someone my size.

Raffles Hotel

What's this? A lawn for bears like me to play on???
No, it's the Bar and Billiard Room at the Raffles Hotel. What, does he also have his own hotel?
Actually no, he doesn't. This incredibly beautiful hotel was named the year
a memorial of Raffles was inaugurated in Singapore. It's such a fabulous place.
Up and down great staircases, across tropical gardens, up onto verandas that take you
straight to the cricket pitch I'm playing on now :). I wasn't allowed into the famous
Long Bar because apparently I'm too short to be allowed in ...!

I argued and argued and then argued some more but no way could I enter the Long Bar.

This is probably the most famous hotel in Asia, though it is more like a little town to me with its juice bars, shops, restaurants and bakeries. The hotel has such a great history and the list of famous film stars staying here is longer than a toilet roll. The hotel opened in 1887, that's a long time ago, right, so you can imagine the amount of funny stories about the place. One was about a tiger hiding under the billiard table and scared just about everyone until it was taken away in the early hours of the morning by an Englishman who came in his pyjamas. :))

So I tried to sneak in through the back door. :)

A horse, a horse,
my kingdom for a horse ...!
I really want this cool horse.

Tucked away like we little bears usually are, is a treasure trove of fantastic antique toys. The Children's Little Museum that lies near to the Sultan Mosque shows you just what mum and dad used to play with before you were born. There are also toys that boys and girls made for themselves. It's amazing! Wish toy shops were like this today!

With the mosque in the background and the palace to the right, this is a really stunning place.

the Arab quarters

Look,
I'm Aladdin!
On my very own
'magic carpet'.
Now, let's go and find
that lamp?

I just ran across a field after being chased by chess pieces (from a cemetery),
jumped on a magic carpet and arrived here in the Arab quarters.
Wow! It's bright, colourful and there is an aroma of delicious food in the air.

Kampong Glam was a thriving port town back in the day around 1822 and was the home
of Malay royalty. The port was so busy with traders, many coming from Yemen in the
Middle East, that it became known as Arab Street. The Sultan Mosque was built here to
cater for the growing Muslim population — right next to the Malay Royal Palace, now the
Malay Heritage Centre. You have to go inside to see an amazing collection of historical goodies.

N

It looks more like a fruitcake or a palace than a museum.

National Museum of Singapore

... And you get to the fabulous National Museum of Singapore that looks like a magical palace.
This is not just any old museum — but a building packed full of the history of Singapore.
It started off as a library and grew like a pumpkin into a huge treasure trove with
amazing educational and multi-media presentations. I spent five hours walking and learning,
wide-eyed around this place and then came across PLAY@NMS. So I did, I played my heart out.

I'm not kidding, this place is great.

How are you supposed to read this school report?

14

M

While at the Museum, try to find a stone, a small fragment of a larger boulder that was discovered many years ago. It is inscribed with writing that dates back to the 10th century. That means there were people living here long ago! When clearing through the jungle to build a road, a group of workmen came across this huge boulder with the funny writing on it. They got scared and ran for their lives believing it was a demon's gateway. Even today, nobody knows what it says. See if you can decipher the secret of the Singapore Stone.

* Now I'm really tired, it must be my bedtime. But first I have to drag myself across to the fantastic Singapore Art Museum nearby. I need my supper of 'arty' sandwiches. :))

15

WOW!
There are more colours here than in a tube of Smarties.

Wow! I've fallen right into a colour palette. The Indians really do brighten places up.
I was told that Indian convicts were sent here to work and given this plot of land by
the British many years ago. With the Serangoon River running right next to it, it was
a great place for raising cattle, and they started trading in livestock. Today, it is still
a bustling place with wonderful shops, great food and everyone looking happy.
And I know why... It's all the wonderful colour. :)

Little INDIA

If you want to see something different, try and see the festival of Thaipusam. It does not look like a party to me, no it does not, but these Hindu devotees seem to be having fun. Unfortunately (or fortunately for some followers), this event only happens once a year and always under a full moon, in either January and February. The Thaipusam festival celebrates a time when Murugan, the Hindu God of War, was given a spear by Parvati, the God of love, to stop the evil demon Soorapadam from running around crazily and hurting people.

I also saw a wedding. The guests threw water over the couple, I thought it was going to be much more colourful. :)

Are you kidding me!
That's a telephone?

I love Emerald Hill Road.
It looks half natural, half man-made,
with a dash of sparkly colour.

Just across from Orchard Road is the old Fort Canning and I am back to greenery and trees. :) There is not much left of the old Fort today except some walls and the entrance gate, but it does have some whacky underground tunnels to explore and it is the home of the Battle Box. The Battle Box was the British Army's World War Two underground operations building that they used before surrendering to the Japanese. Oh, I feel like 007! And is that really what a telephone used to look like?

This road is just too long.
I wonder if they will let me on a bus.

ORCHARD Road

It's very likely you will find yourself here on Orchard Road (I think because mum and dad would like to visit this place more than you or me). This long and ultra modern road is lined with more shopping malls than a box of Lego bricks, but there are great attractions for us if you can find them between the shops and restaurants. Just off Orchard Road is beautiful Emerald Hill Road. Here is what Singapore looked like nearly 100 years ago. Can you imagine that back then, this road was a humble dirt lane that passed through orchards and plantations growing fruit, nutmeg and pepper on either side. Look at it NOW!

SINGAPORE
BOTANIC GARDENS

Ooooohh! This place is cool, really cool. I mean soooo cool.

When the park first opened in 1859, it was used to cultivate the rubber plant (the stuff they make car tyres from) as rubber had a big economic value at the time. Later on people donated animals to the park and soon these gardens had loads of animals walking around. Among the animals were two big Sumatran Rhinos who allowed people to stroke and feed them. But when they were hungry they would both start to squeak and this scared people off. I thought only mice squeaked?

This was the best idea I've had, sitting and relaxing under the orchid flowers.

I got my sandwiches and came running over to the beautiful Singapore Botanic Gardens for a picnic. This place is filled with stunning nature and an amazing orchid garden; orchids are the national flower of Singapore. It's also really big and I get SO hot with this furry coat on. But, I can always run over to the Cool House because it's just that COOL. Haaaa! Honestly though, for you and me, the best place in the gardens is the Jacob Ballas Children's Garden. Here you can learn about and discover the importance of plants and nature. It is also a good place to get my paws wet. :)

Jacob was not thinking of me when he made this park. Look! I can't even reach the handle.

牛车水
Niu Che Shui

You've been following me around all day Mr Monkey...

A cow that drives a water cart! That is the amazing name in Chinese for Chinatown!
Nearly 200 years ago, more than 100,000 Chinese left their homes in China to find their fortune
in Singapore. They set up restaurants and bazaars, operated theatres or simply helped their families in
a new land. They were known as 'an industrious race'. I don't know what that means but it sounds fast.
Chinatown has many heritage sites — which means you can't mess about with them — so it
looks very much like it did 100 years ago. The buildings are beautiful, so colourful, and the
architectural forms are exquisite. That is probably why the buildings are called 'Painted Ladies'. :)

22

Taxi! Taxi! What you see here is a taxi. Yep! An old world taxi. Before the car existed, people would travel around this part of Asia on rickshaws or trishaws. Back in the good old days, this was the only form of public transport. Previously, rickshaws used to be pulled by men holding two bars and running. It was cheap, but really hard for the coolies who pulled them until the invention of the bicycle. In the 1980s, it was still easy to hire a trishaw in Singapore, but now they have nearly all disappeared. Such a shame, I kind of like them. At least I can try this one.

So, this is what it must have looked like not that many years ago. My, how things have changed. No water carts now.

Hungry Bears' Hawker Centre

Lau Pa Sat

Can you smell that? Can you? Welcome to food lovers' Disneyland, housed in the most beautiful cathedral-like building. The site was originally a wet market designed by George Coleman. Some years later it was moved to this location and a Scottish guy called MacRitchie put in the final touches. Remember his name as he appears often. The best thing about Singapore is its multicultural society which means, here especially, that you can eat whatever you want from around the world and it is all so yummy. But leave room for dessert and some shaved ice. Yes, shaved ice! It cools me down and looks fantastic, like my paintings. :)

24

On a hot day, OK, everyday is
a hot day, it is so cool to visit
this great building for a shaved ice.

What are wet markets? The difference between a dry and a wet market is simple and it makes sense once you know why. A traditional wet market sells live animals, vegetables and in some cases, flowers. The animals are checked by the customers before being killed and sold. The slaughter causes an amazing yucky mess that has to be cleaned up. Everything is washed down and cleaned with water. The meat, the vegetables and even the flowers got a watering too. They also turned the hoses on me and watered me down. :(I think I'll go to a dry market next time and look at the radios.

Just let me get this straight,
are you a whale or a fish?

25

The water from the rain comes down through the ceiling and falls into a well. And that water is also used in the toilet. :)

Being in a museum is not one of my favourite things, but this has got to be the most different. Wherever you look there is something great going on. I had a wonderful time in the workshop learning new things. I admit I was super happy beating my friend at building the best cosmic super rocket.

Can you see the similarity between the lotus flower and this building?

26

Hello! Aren't you upside down?

The Lotus Flower
ARTSCIENCE MUSEUM

OMG. I've wondered for weeks about this building. What is it? A space ship? Picasso's hand? Or a lotus flower? It is actually the ArtScience Museum at Marina Bay Sands. This incredible building is home to spectacular exhibitions showcasing art and science. It is also designed to be environmentally friendly and collects water and electricity through its roof. So if you go to the toilet, turn on the light and flush the chain, it all comes straight from the roof. So cool! That reminds me, I need a pee!

The best slide in the world.
(Only for bears though, hahaha!)

MARINA BARRAGE

And it doesn't get more interesting than Marina Barrage. Did you know Marine Barrage
is a reservoir, but not just any old reservoir though. It is also a playing field, a water light show,
a concert hall under the sky, a kite flying paradise and is also brilliant for picnics.
And just look at the fabulous multi-coloured views of wonderful Singapore! The best
bit though is that there is nearly always a breeze here. My fur feels dry for once. :)

I honestly did not know there were so many forms of kites. It is like a alien world in the sky.

The barrage stops the water from flooding the area at high tide by squirting out an Olympic-pool-size volume of water EVERY MINUTE.

Do you know how big an Olympic-size pool is? Enormous! More or less 5,000,000 of these bottles.

500ml

Ah, but the real interesting bit is this. The Marina Barrage is also a dam and keeps parts of Singapore from flooding. It separates the rainwater from the sea water and keeps the water at a constant level so I can enjoy a little paddle surf by myself, without those nuisance waves. I could write pages about this place, but you will get a much better idea about how it all works at the Sustainable Singapore Gallery.

I am going to love this.
Can we get on a yellow one????

There is a very special way to get to Sentosa Island and that is to fly, but not in a plane. You can take a cable car ride across. You can get on at Mount Faber and ride the skies looking down at everything below. It really does go quite high up here and the views of the city are fantastic. Look at all those boats out on the sea. If you go at dusk, the hundreds of boats look like a flat city with all their lights on.

Look, it's a city that floats.

Harbour Front
Maritime Square

30

Come on, let's see what is going on around here. I am walking towards the Harbour Front Centre which is near to Mount Faber. Singapore has been known as a major shipping trade port for such a long time now and right here at Keppel Harbour was where the Port of Singapore started with sail boats and steam ships galore. Today, this is the world's busiest port and where we are going now will show you exactly how busy this great big port actually is. Now for the the long crooked walk up lush Mount Faber.

Surfing like a Pro!
And no one even checked to see
if I am wearing swimmers. :)

So this is ATTRACTION city.
After my swim I looked around and you would not believe it...
from aquariums to roller coasters to log flumes and a luge trail
down the hill, there is everything. It is so much fun!
But what I really wanted to do was try my furry paws at
surfing. What?! I am a cool bear! That was splashing, it was.
Now I have to dry my wet furry bum before dinner.

Are they spacemen leaving earth?
That looks really weird, but fun.

SENTOSA ISLAND

Is the castle in there?

Sit, and dip your toes in the water on Sentosa. Yes, a beach! For the first time, I feel like I am on holiday. :) This island has incredible attractions for everyone but I will get to that in a minute. Before it was called Sentosa, the island was known as Pulau Blakang Mati which translates as 'Death Island'. Scary! Some say it was called this because of the fighting between pirates. :0 Anyway, in 1971, they decided to hold a competition for a new name. One person suggested Tranquillity — which is what Sentosa means in Malay — and won. Hurray! Funnily enough though, they were actually thinking of turning the island into a huge oil refinery, but a clever government economist said there was more money to be made in making things fun! Hurray, again!

Kampong Buangkok

Tabby thinks
the roof needs
re-doing.
I kind of like it.

Hmmm! Fresh air. Let's go back in time and have a look at Singapore life in the 1950s.
Kampong Lorong Buangkok has not changed since then. It's a jungle village and
I feel at home here. There are old wooden houses with metal zinc roofs.

There is no organised structure and a grateful lack of signposts. Wow, so different from
Orchard Road. But, why is this tranquil place not filled with artists? Well, because this
area floods quite often during the rainy monsoon season. The village was known as
Kampong Selak Kain which means 'pull your sarong (skirt) up' in Malay. Isn't that great?

Quick, jump, run for your lives! There's a dragon spitting slides.

We are going to go somewhere really special for people my size. Well OK, your size too. There is a dragon in Singapore that is really special and no one knows how long he will stay. Welcome to the Toa Payoh children's playground. Most mums and dads from Singapore would have played with these dragons, but now, they are considered too dangerous and the dragons are leaving. Such a shame, he really is a very nice dragon.

Too much water...
When it rains, wear a bikini?

Up in the sky, balancing on planks, tight ropes and moving platforms, until the dreaded death slide!

Swinging through the trees like Tarzan has got to be the most fun a bear can have! If you are an adventure junkie like me, then this is something you really should try. It is an obstacle course set high in the treetops of the Bedok Reservoir. Gather all your courage as you go whizzing through the trees, navigate across ladders, bridges, swinging planks, and zip right across a reservoir. It's so much fun, but do watch out for that gorilla. He is insane!

Forest Adventure

... But the adventure does not stop there. The Forest Adventure playground sits by Bedok Reservoir, and next to it is the Water Venture. If you have ever wanted to race a boat in a group or simply indulge in some leisurely kayaking with friends or family, this is the place. I saw dragon boats sailing into the distance as well but what I saw a lot of were people getting wet too. Surely, that has got to be fun, no?

Not quite my size, is it?

The word bumboat comes from the Dutch word for canoe, 'boomschuit'.

Pulau Ubin

I am happiest in nature because I am a bear. For me this is a highlight of my adventure through Singapore and it starts here because I get to go on a bumboat. Hahaha! A fantastic boat trip to an island of yesteryear. Pulau Ubin has a great network of dirt roads under overgrown rubber plantations for walking or you can hire a bicycle. It also has a boardwalk through the mangroves, a fantastic array of special birds and of course, wonderful people. The air is fresher here and the noise is ... where is the NOISE???

What is wrong with dogs???
I asked him the way to the
quarry, politely, and he just
growled at me ...

BICYCLES

:))
This is
bike city guys.

If you are allowed to hire a bike, you have to cycle up to the old quarries. This island was known to the Malays as the Granite Stone Island. All over Singapore you can see floor tiles in the buildings that are made from the granite of this island. The word tile in Malay is Jubin which now explains why the island is called Ubin. Where has the 'J' gone? Watch out for a hornbill with its funky yellow beak.

39

Listen tiger!
You can meow all you want,
but my teeth will always be
cleaner than yours.

IMMIGRATION SINGAPORE
VISIT PASS
Subject to Reg. 12 (7)
Immigration Regulations

- 15 APR 2016

PERMITTED TO ENTER AND
REMAIN IN SINGAPORE
FOR NINETY DAYS FOR
SOCIAL VISIT ONLY FROM
DATE SHOWN ABOVE

I saw two baboons
grooming each other.
Actually, I saw lots of
them and was told this
is a sign of friendship.
It is like giving a hug to
your best friend. So
much to learn and see.
Talking about seeing
things, what can you see
at the Night Safari?

Singapore
ZOO

Oops! It looks like Bill and Ben did not get enough to eat...

Shall we have breakfast with my friends, the orang utans? Or, as we are here early,
would you like to listen to the incredible boom of a Siamang monkey. This monkey's
morning call can be heard miles away. He's very funny and so is that pouch on his neck.
This is a place where everyone can have a wild time.

If you are a night owl or a sleep walker do not miss a trip to the Night Safari. You see so many strange animals at night here but one really stands out for me. A mouse-deer is a cross between a small mouse and a huge deer. How did that happen? What a funny looking animal.

Watch your head carefully for flying foxes or flying squirrels! It seems that at night most of these animals here go absolutely bonkers! It is funtastic and you can forget about sleeping!

Alright Mr Flying Fox, tell me, is it because you are too top heavy being upside down all the time?

I really cannot believe it. The elephants were scared of me. No way could I get on them. Why, I am just a bear?

42

Wildlife
RESERVES
Singapore Zoo

I am home, no really I am. It is not a zoo, it is a world. There are four parks here, all different and it would take a whole book to write about it. A Zoo, River Safari, Jurong Bird Park and a Night Safari. You know you human beings are the animals here. :) Try and find Ranger Ooz whilst you are here. You will learn something from him. Honest!

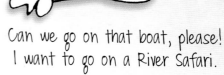

Can we go on that boat, please! I want to go on a River Safari.

I am so glad I do not wear a watch because you have to be soooo patient when fishing.

Let us go prawning. To put it simply, prawning is fishing for those horrible water dinosaurs that mum and dad love to eat. Yep, prawns, yuck! But it is fun. I haven't been fishing for some time so my abilities have regressed a little. They gave me a rod with a line and I sat, and sat, and sat and then I caught one. :) It was massive, no way am I picking up that beast. Oh well, back to pawing salmon out of the river.

I could not believe my eyes. A bright red bird lying on a bed, without a care in the world.

IMMIGRATION SINGAPORE
VISIT PASS
Subject to Reg. 12 (7)
Immigration Regulations
– 15 APR 2016
PERMITTED TO ENTER
REMAIN IN SINGAPORE
FOR NINETY DAYS
SOCIAL VISIT ONLY
DATE SHOWN ABOVE ONLY

What is wrong puppy, have you never seen a grown bear before?

FARMART

Countryside friends! I have come to a funny kind of supermarket with an edge to it. Oh wow! The place is packed with animals you can actually feed and there are newly laid eggs to buy. You can learn so much about farm life here. You can also go and play with the koi fish and feed them as well. They have the biggest mouths, I was scared stiff with fright. The puppies barked at me as I passed. I cannot imagine why?

Whee!
I'm flying above
the trees.

Now this is wild, really wild! A 250-metre long suspended bridge over a rainforest canopy. I feel like a bird looking down at all the wildlife and vegetation below. When you reach the middle of the bridge hold up your arms and look all around at this awesome scenery for a moment. Only then will you realise that the bridge is actually swaying! I love it. Home sweet home! I have to be careful not to get my paws stuck in the metal grate though.

MacRitchie
Tree Top Walk

I know he is coming...
but when he is really close I will turn
around and growl my biggest GROWL :))

Have you seen this crazy guy?
What an amazing bird.

Hi, I have just been talking to a racket-tailed drongo. Bet you do not know what it is, do you?
Wow this is a tough walk and I am sweating lots. From all the dazzle of the city into a tree lined daze.
Where am I? There isn't a single building in sight here, just trees, plants and birds.
It is incredible. Here, I am in a real rainforest. Here, at MacRitchie, I have seen all kinds
of animals from lizards (massive ones) to beautiful birds and monkeys everywhere.
If you look around, this is what the whole of Singapore looked like 150 years ago. A jungle!

Bridges
of Singapore

I know, it is a funny subject, but I am a bear. We tend to forget the importance of bridges.
Bridges unite people, socially and culturally. They are like a handshake, they connect both
ways and you can always see a smile from the person in front. They are also incredibly
intricate in design and engineering and many are very beautiful. Here in Singapore
there are so many bridges connecting places and people, that you start to
understand the wonders of this intricate mixture of people!
Welcome to Singapore!

Hanging on for dear life here,
but what a whacky wavey bridge.

I just love this bicycle, sorry, bridge.
It is like an enormous playground.

IMMIGRATION SINGAPORE
VISIT PASS
Subject to Reg. 12 (7)
Immigration Regulations

- 15 APR 2016

PERMITTED TO ENTER AND
REMAIN IN SINGAPORE
FOR NINETY DAYS FOR
SOCIAL VISIT FROM
DATE SHOWN ABOVE.

Sorry guys, I have to talk about the beauty of bridges and this one,
Cavanagh Bridge, looks like it is laced with a bicycle chain. Its elegant and
simple design is like plaited string. Being the first and only suspension
bridge on the island, it became overloaded with increasing traffic, too many
carts and rickshaws. Stop! So today, it is just my paws and a leisurely walk
across. It is funny that Cavanagh Bridge also solved the problem of stopping
sailboats going up the river because it was too low. :)

21

Someone told me this was the very frst iPod... hahahaha, no way!

baba house

Just look at that blue! Baba House belonged to a very prominent Peranakan family. Peranakan means 'descendant', and Peranakan families were usually Chinese descendants but not always. They were well-skilled traders, most of whom spoke at least two languages. Their families call themselves Baba Nyonya. 'Baba' means 'gentleman' and because many traders had no wives, they intermarried here with the local women, 'Nyonya', meaning 'lady', hence Baba Nyonya. Great name. Let us go in because you're going to love this.

Don't you think it looks like a doll's house?

When I walked into this amazing house, my first thought was that it was an elaborate doll's house but for humans. The decoration, colour, detail and culture is absolutely amazing. Most Peranakan dwellings respect the concept of 'Feng Shui'. Wood, fire, earth, metal and water are the main elements everywhere; Feng Shui is all about balancing the energy in a building, a certain harmony. Ensuring good fortune, health and luck.

A see-saw, that is what I need to understand what this Feng Shui business is all about. Balance!

This temple looks like a boat to me with its amazing colour, shape and carved wooden panels. At night, the temple looks like a wonderful Christmas cake, but go inside and you will be amazed. Apart from being grand you cannot stop looking at every little detail. Look for the 99 golden dragons, every one of them different. Why 99 and not a 100? Because in Chinese culture, the number nine is considered very lucky. Now, try and find a small, red envelope. If you can have one, take one. They say that parents put money in them at New Year or on birthdays. Cross your fingers!

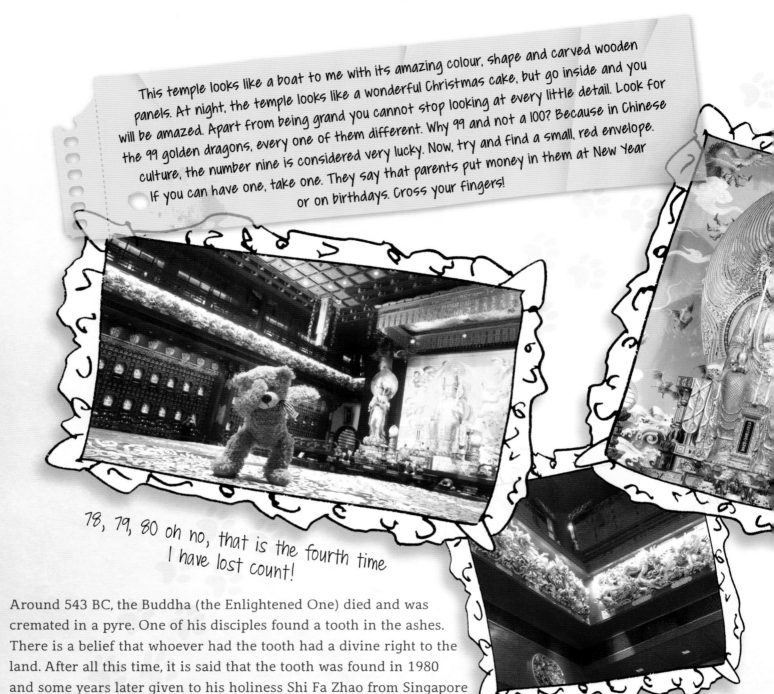

78, 79, 80 oh no, that is the fourth time I have lost count!

Around 543 BC, the Buddha (the Enlightened One) died and was cremated in a pyre. One of his disciples found a tooth in the ashes. There is a belief that whoever had the tooth had a divine right to the land. After all this time, it is said that the tooth was found in 1980 and some years later given to his holiness Shi Fa Zhao from Singapore as the new guardian of the precious relic. He was told that if possible he should build a monastery for the Sacred Buddha Tooth Relic. And that is where I have come today. Do you think it's true that Buddha's 2,500-year-old tooth is kept inside? Mudley the secret agent goes to investigate.

Buddha Tooth Relic Temple

Hey, calm down! What is wrong with baked beans for lunch?

Gosh! How big was his tooth? This place is a massive palace !!!

The River

Singapore River

Fancy a dip? The wonderful Singapore River has a fascinating history. It was here that this great.. what is it, a city? an island? a country? sprang from the riverbed into what Singapore is today. It was here where the main port used to be and quickly became the centre for trade. Many years ago you could hardly see the water because of the bumboats tied to the shore. Thousands of them, packed together just like a huge tin of sardines.

Excuse me, I am looking for my boat.
It is brown with a green awning ...???

In the 1970s and 1980s, Singapore, like most other countries, was happily demolishing anything old to replace with the new, but the city came on hard times economically and the wrecking stopped, much to the happiness of many. The old warehouses and shop fronts were seen to be particularly symbolic of Singapore's heritage and the decision was made to keep the beautiful old buildings and change it into this.

The best thing is that they have been turned into restaurants.
Yum, I am hungry! Garçon, please, spare this bear a penny for food.

Oh, come on guys. Stop looking so grumpy, it is only a photo with ME!

Ouch! That is a horrible tree

gardens
BY THE BAY

Gosh, I really have my mouth wide open at this sight. These awesome magical gardens take your breath away. This is a massive world garden filled with inspirational ideas. These two domes work like ecosystems — one for the Mediterranean plant life and the other for mountainous plant life (because the higher you are, the harsher the climate is). The amount of colour here puts my paintings to shame.

Come on girls, don't be scared.
Look at me, no hands. haha!

These two incredibly big glass domes are really called 'Biomes'. What they do is sustain in one a dry arid climate whilst in the other a moist (it is quite cold, so take a jacket) climate. The special glass that they use lets in all the light but keeps out the heat (not like mum and dads' car). The dead leaves go into a furnace to create ash fertiliser that is then given to seedlings. Isn't that amazing. :))

Fat trees everyone,
fantastically funny fat trees.

Everything is so spiky from here. Amazing!

This, my dear friends is a symbol of man working with nature in the best possible way. These 18 Supertrees are actually vertical gardens. They work just like real trees by gathering sunlight from their solar panels for the brilliant light show at night and to pump out the dirty air from the nearby conservatories and suck in clean air to put back in. They also collect rainwater that is then used to water the plants inside the conservatories. Isn't that a fascinating tree, made by man?

Incredible tree. Nuff said!

SUPERTREES
by the bay

You will get a much better look by strolling along the Skywalk Bridge, located 25 metres above the ground. By the way, there is also an great garden for bears and kids like us, which is great... for getting wet! :))

Hey guys, wait for me ...

This place is like another planet. Oh, hang on, it is another planet!

So all the water collected from those trees water the plants in here.

I wonder if he has noticed where I am getting my clay from? I hope not!

The Wonders of Sculpture

Gees! I thought I would never get here, but I have and it seems I am late. :)
This is my friend Fah Cheong, a well-known sculptor from Singapore.
Although he has a lot of his work in public places here, he also has his sculptures in
many other countries. I am so lucky to work with him on this sculpture of a young boy
on a bicycle. Or am I just happy to be messing around with all this clay?
Look at Fah Cheong, so intense, but he seems to be loving it.

Anybody got a chisel made for my paws??

I think sculpture is amazing because you can create it using so many different materials. There are two aspects to this wonderful art: one is carving, which means 'removing of the material' like with granite or wood and the other is modelling, which means 'adding to the material', like clay or plaster. Whether it's made of metal, stone, wood or anything else, it is a marvellous visual art in three dimensions. Sometimes you spot one, sometimes they sculptures around Singapore. Sometimes you spot one, sometimes they blend into the landscape, but remember: behind every sculpture there are the hands of an artist. :)

When you walk around Singapore you will see lots of sculptures, like this one from Fah Cheong. Brilliant!

The End

What a thrill to have spent time here. I have loved being in Singapore but now
I'm going for a swim, then pack my bags, catch my plane and head off to my next destination.
My sculptor friend has told me all about the wonderful art and culture of Mud Town.
I'm looking forward to that. I hope Sophie likes what I've seen and learnt
from Singapore. I can't wait to tell her all about it.

See you soon Lion City. Good bye!
And I hope to share the secrets of Kuala Lumpur with you shortly,
Your friend,
Mudley

Follow the paws!
There is a beautiful and
wonderful world out there...

See you next time!

About the Author

Born to English parents, Arp Raph Broadhead lived his first 12 years in Africa and later in Papua New Guinea. He studied Art and Design at the College of Art, Manchester University, England and presently lives and works between Vigo, Spain, and New York, USA. His art and designs have been exhibited/shown in many countries around the world and he continues to search for innovative solutions whether in furniture, mobility devices or his paintings.

© 2016 Arp Raph Broadhead and Marshall Cavendish International (Asia) Pte Ltd

Published by Marshall Cavendish Editions
Marshall Cavendish Editions is an imprint of Marshall Cavendish International
1 New Industrial Road, Singapore 536196

Other Marshall Cavendish Offices:
Marshall Cavendish Corporation. 99 White Plains Road, Tarrytown NY 10591-9001, USA • Marshall Cavendish International (Thailand) Co Ltd. 253 Asoke, 12th Flr, Sukhumvit 21 Road, Klongtoey Nua, Wattana, Bangkok 10110, Thailand • Marshall Cavendish (Malaysia) Sdn Bhd, Times Subang, Lot 46, Subang Hi-Tech Industrial Park, Batu Tiga, 40000 Shah Alam, Selangor Darul Ehsan, Malaysia.

Marshall Cavendish is a trademark of Times Publishing Limited

National Library Board, Singapore Cataloguing-in-Publication Data
Name(s): Broadhead , Arp Raph.
Title: Mudley explores Singapore : an amazing adventure in the Lion City / Arp Raph Broadhead.
Description: Singapore : Marshall Cavendish Editions, 2016.
Identifier(s): OCN 948339519 | ISBN 978-981-47-2195-0 (paperback)
Subject(s): LCSH: Singapore—Description and travel—Juvenile literature. | Singapore—History—Juvenile literature.
Classification: DDC 915.95704—dc23

Printed in Singapore by Fabulous Printers Pte Ltd